EMOTES

NAGMA SHAIK

Made with ❤ on the Notion Press Platform
www.notionpress.com

to the moments (smile and gaze into the distance).

Contents

Foreword   *vii*

1. Why?   1

2. Early Morning Star   2

3. Unspoken Truth   3

4. The Sound Of Night   4

5. Twirl Of A Feeling   5

6. Beginning   6

7. Infatuation Or Love?   7

8. Stillness   8

9. Sky   9

10. Sleep   10

11. The Silence   11

12. After – End   13

13. Ocean Dawn   14

14. Rain   15

15. Unturned Pages   16

16. Balance   17

17. Exposure   18

18. Pure   19

19. She   20

20. Passing By   21

21. Era   22

22. A Friend   23

Foreword

ride starting in 3...2.....

1. Why?

You ; A beautiful feeling just like the distant sky ,

Lost in your deep crystal eyes when the sunlight hits just right ,

As the waves rest on shore feels like I need your touch more ,

Like a rainy day you make me happy in every way ;

Fine line between love and infatuation ,

Either way both are volatile ,

Your dreamy in those bedroom eyes,

Driving me insanely out of my mind ,

But I wouldn't want it in any another way ;

I close my eyes , take a deep sigh ,

And let you see my vacant eyes ;

Just like darkness takes over the night sky.

2. Early MORNING STAR

I have written a handful of thoughts in my mind time and again;
Only imaginable the way its supposed to be,
Still patiently waiting what nature has to offer today.
Dusky morning, blurry eyes with one stretch everything getting clear;
Jumping right up to see the desired sunrise, running up to the terrace
Beamed at my favourite spot at the topmost summit of my domicile;
There I sat all relaxed and recoiled waiting patiently looking up at the sky,
Well I was eager to see the beauty which had caused me to go a little early,
Time is passing by every minute with the longing of empyrean,
Fresh breeze, chirpy birds, blissful sky.
Wild blue yonder ever changing,
Astonished by each painting,
Amidst all the calmness, rises the sun like a cocoon breakthrough;
Spreading its rays comes out an amber circlet.
Birds wavering around and here I am with inner peace and elation,
Bliss of admiring the panoramic view of the creation.

3. Unspoken TRUTH

• 3 •

Its just not the way it never was,
Can't fake myself for a cause,
Can't fake myself for a applause
It's not easy and it never was.
I have been real much forgotten the sound of applause,
People can't handle real cause, they can't take the reality clause,
It's not facile and it never was.
Let's just take a pause,
Feel the fervour, feel the personage,
Cause at the end, fake take the applause.

4. The sound of NIGHT

Night sky is so calming,
Surrounded with darkness so soothing;
Lying down eyes lost in the dark,
Looking for the night to spark;
With no ounce of sleep,
Lost in wilderness so deep;
Imagining my fantasies come to life; on the ceiling height,
Sometimes I sound a creep,
In actual silence is all I greed;
Which gives me immense peace,
Is the eolion tones of the breeze;
With all the loud mess in my head,
Some great conversations were held;
Preferred comfortable silence under the sky over a fancy dinner plate,
Maybe love is about fate;
So is my thought of ideal night date;
Just a peculiar soul, with infatuation to being a romantique
Coming to a final yet:
A quite ecstasy in an oblivion state.

5. Twirl of a FEELING

I can't find words when I talk,

Framing a sentence tends to be a task;

Aghast on how imminent my written thoughts forever are;

For a brief sense of moment we come together,

And when it's gone we fall back to blankness;

A sonnet of chemical hearts,

Fondness for love under a sky full of stars;

Often I romanticize every poem,

Like lost in the gaze of exquisite nature letting out a quiesce moan;

Undoubtedly perceive romance without a caress.

6. BEGINNING

I know him but,know not who he is,
Once in a blue moon I pinged you,
That day who knew;
Nattered for a bit far along,
Never knew we would get along,
Crossed paths contrarily,
Thought it would be temporary;
Until one twilight we met;
Sauntered around for a short amount,
Silence of the night mocking at our first sound,
With twinkling smiles we bid adieu,
Wishing to see more of you.

7. INFATUATION or LOVE?

Over and over again we met,

Not gratified yet; Will I ever?

Every time was an adventure,

Clear hazel eyes, jest laugh, it lightly grazed my heart;

I saw your passion gleam,

In my chaos you were calming,

Maybe it was an infatuation.

Until we bid adieu without a conclusion,

In no time you were gone,

Left me wondering our encounters all along;

When I talked out my emote;

I realised you had moved out.

Oh amour! That was a heck of a ride;

Like a five feet apart tide,

Almost an unfathomable end.

8. STILLNESS

I write what I cannot hold back,
For a while left it on pause,
Hoping not a certain feeling,
Just a long stare,vaguely blinking,
In my head words start appealing,
To put an end to that urge of speaking,
Everything that's missing,
In that very stillness,
I waved hello to the moon,
In a state of blankness.

9. SKY

Every time I gaze up,

Do I love the moving clouds?

Do I love the peace it gives with the poignant passing?

Do I love the sky with every colour it changes with the passing time?

Do I love dusk to dawn?

Do I love just the romantic sunset or the early sunrise?

Do I love the moment when I embrace love looking in the distant blue sky?

Do I love the time I seek for your forgiveness?

Do I love the rain through or the blissful sunlight?

Every time I seek answers to the situations you put me through I still look up,

With every I feel I look up,

With every question I look up and still be etonne,

With every iota of peace, a moment of relief I get by looking up is the time I realise

I do! Did and will even if it's a little ounce.

This is what I will always be obsessed,

What the sky has to canvas about?

10. SLEEP

On sleepless nights, I write;

Words keep me accompanied

Like a night light,

Sky filled distant stars that spark,

Giving hope in dark;

As much it pleads peace,

Keeps me filled with thoughts;

Ah! Silly that I need silence dark, to finally close my eyes;

Turning every passing minute to a cravingly endless warm hug.

11. The SILENCE

The time she could feel every sound,
With a leaping bound;
Every sense could feel the loss of control,
See-through darkness probing for more;
Just as the eyes are close,
There is nothing but Eigengrau to expose,
Back of her mind fantasies commence,
To a place of untold sense;
In her sub-conscience, she awakens amidst
the wilderness that she adored;
A wet upthrust lead to an epiphany,
Afloat she was in the ocean's melodious symphony;
A soak in stagnancy, silence possessed around;
Gust gliding in caressing every inch,
Verdure filled like a serene clinch;
Somewhere in the distant sky,
Birds conversing in their flocks,
Awaiting to get drenched are the rocks,
As they lay reflecting gleams of daylight;
Lonesome she wished for a soul beside,
Just when a fish sneaked a jump by her side,
Filled with chiliadal souls, never was she alone;
Isn't the silence so calming,
Quite embracing,
When she opened her eyes,

Heart couldn't contain her joy,
To yet an another night stay, someday.

12. AFTER – END

Lost in nothing at last,

Now get me off this rollercoaster,

Looking paused, not to be a lost cause;

Of all the pain,

Vacuous mind in vain,

Hurt filled scar, an embracing mark;

Lost with hope, love with cope;

Silence taking over each gaze,

Carrying the pieces through a maze,

Compassionate vulnerability to a weathered heart.

13. OCEAN DAWN

Walking on the shore with warm sand seep in my toes,
With every lift like an hour glass,
The lightness soothing the pain off my waist;
As I fall back by the shore,
A sense of relief gushes with every surge of tide,
Sparkling waves in an endless loop hit back every inch like a jolt;
Just when at ease are my emotions,
It's almost dawn amour;
Amber reflection painting a polaroid film,
Calm entangled breeze, juniper luscious tropics closing in,
Tormenting hopeless romantic,
In that very moment my soul was alive;
Falling yet again for a perfect emote.

14. RAIN

As I breathe the scent of rain,
I let go a sigh of my pain;
Droplets creating a melody,
Enclosed in nature's remedy;
Soothing my skin is cold breeze,
Elated nature is a tease;
This moment sky is feeling blue and grey,
Delightful are the soul's astray;
Love seeks warm embrace,
Sorrow leans to find grace;
Hidden mist in surrounding,
Oh! That's a mystery astonishing;
Hope peeping through the end,
Oh rain, you made the dawn rise again.

15. UNTURNED PAGES

A kid started a journal;
Wrote every bit of feel,
Sometimes to talk other times to heal,
Emotions overwhelmed within,
Still wishing to be understood,
Scribbled little details, unravelling lost thoughts,
As time passed with every fading memory in short,
Heap of diaries in a forgotten form,
At last left with dust to mourn,
A gazing stone image,
An empath, wishing to be understood.

16. BALANCE

I have a charcoal and a paint side,
One overpowering the other,
Contained in an hourglass of breath;
Voyaging in to dark abyss of ocean,
Caressing the opaque and yet translucency of water,
I could fantasize or just open my eyes to the flamboyant chiliadial
souls;
Heightened postulation of thoughtfulness,
The poet controlling my emotions, the painter swaying my soul,
Coaxed my body to oblivion;
Thou hail me out of the space when I am thinking straight,
Just not yet.

17. EXPOSURE

Stay silent mind,
While eyes keep shouting,
Need you to be composed,
Don't want my heart to be exposed;
Your not trying enough,
It's never enough.

18. PURE

It was just a touch,
That was over-much,
The sense that lead to a crumbled ache;
I poured my heart out, thou were all ears,
I got vulnerable, a sight to endear;
Curves coaxed me to a dead end,
My genre allured an eternity,
Unavailing with consumed love,
Seeking passion alongside adventure,
Over and over a path envisioned,
Words put together to find an good end.

19. SHE

She shut down those thoughts,
She tried and fought,
She is getting older,
She is making nothingness her friend much bolder,
She has become a stranger to herself,
She wants healthy oneself,
She just wanted to confront,
She, for the first time put up a front,
She is screaming,
She is dreaming,
She is hoping,
She is coping,
She needs to be happier and her.
Visualising fantasies in poetry,
Seeking your touch in every line,
Awaiting to make you all mine;
Those bedroom eyes gazing mine,
Losing grip on my body, rising heart and breath;
Don't you just stand there,
I bit my lip to certain depth,
Containing every feel to not pull apart your clothes;
As your stepping close, my thinking was not in control anymore;

20. PASSING by

Pondering growth that's ticking,
More the number ages,
Darkness that is bewildering,
Oh,it's your blinding rage;
Mistaken stages,piling mistakes;
Endless running towards a faint curve,
Let loose rhythm for this take,
Pondered with lack in oeuvres;
A while still scared;
Blankness on white canvas,
Blankness on paper without a care,
Just this nervous,
Finding grip on what's impaired;
Unsaid thoughts,
Lonesome expanse,
Unfolding knots,
Seeking it's beginning to put an end.

21. ERA

Where in time am I lost,

Poetry is mere words and love found in alphabets;

Take me to the aura of hopeless sense,

I won't last a while in this phase.

Counting time,hopeless exercise,

Thinking a waste of time,

Dreaming an endless emotion,

Living a just sound of oxygen,

Take me to the aura of hope,

I am alive,yet gone,

Where in time am I lost.

22. A Friend

Empty place beside me, you filled;

You were a growing seed for a cherry blossom tree,*beautiful and light*;

You turned support to a rosacea creeper seed,*slow and fragile*;

Parallel scarlets of different fruits;

Changing weather never wavered that bond,

We bore witness to varying blooms that was fond,

More than a decade now,

Thankful for the mildest breeze,

Thankful for the joyous shade,

Thankful for the scenery ahead,

Thankful for the chirping adventures unsaid,

Aging alongside just left with branches and stems,

Leaving an artistic gem,

In the peace realm.

Thank you...............................laters